A Rookie reader®

Wrinkles

Written by Pam Miller   Illustrated by Bob Ostrom

Children's Press®
A Division of Scholastic Inc.
New York • Toronto • London • Auckland • Sydney
Mexico City • New Delhi • Hong Kong
Danbury, Connecticut

To Lex, Chris, and Elizabeth,
who are responsible for so many of my favorite
kinds of wrinkles.
— P.M.

For my daughter Mae
— B.O.

Consultant
Eileen Robinson
Reading Specialist

Library of Congress Cataloging-in-Publication Data

Miller, Pamela Anne.
  Wrinkles / written by Pam Miller ;
illustrated by Bob Ostrom.
      p. cm. — (A Rookie reader)
   Summary: Rhyming text and illustrations play with the many meanings
of the word wrinkle.
   ISBN 0-516-24860-X (lib. bdg.)   0-516-25021-3 (pbk.)
   [1. Skin wrinkles—Fiction. 2. Play on words. 3. Stories in rhyme.]
I. Ostrom, Bob, ill. II. Title.
   PZ8.3.M6182Wr 2005
   [E]—dc22
                                2004029834

CHILDREN'S PRESS and A ROOKIE READER®, and associated logos are trademarks
and or registered trademarks of Scholastic Library Publishing. SCHOLASTIC and
associated logos are trademarks and or registered trademarks of Scholastic Inc.
1 2 3 4 5 6 7 8 9 10 R 14 13 12 11 10 09 08 07 06 05

Wrinkles are everywhere!

3

Wrinkles in your brother's shirt,

wrinkles in your sister's skirt.

One sock wrinkles in your shoe,

then the other wrinkles too.

Wrinkles in raisins,

wrinkles in peas.

Wrinkles in elbows,

wrinkles in knees.

Paper wrinkles in a kite.

Elephant wrinkles. What a sight!

A snake leaves wrinkles in the sand.

A bath leaves wrinkles in your hand.

Big, soft wrinkles on your bed.

Lines of wrinkles across your head.

One eye wrinkles,
when someone winks.

22

A nose wrinkles when
something stinks.

Red.

Blue.

Old or new.

We pull. We tug.

We shake them away.

But some wrinkles are here to stay!

Peabody Public Library
Columbia City, IN

Word List (62 Words)
(Words in **bold** are story words that rhyme.)

a	eye	on	**sight**	then
across	**hand**	one	sister's	to
are	**head**	or	**skirt**	**too**
away	here	other	snake	tug
bath	in	paper	sock	we
bed	**kite**	**peas**	soft	what
big	**knees**	pull	some	when
blue	leaves	raisins	someone	**winks**
brother's	lines	red	something	wrinkles
but	**new**	**sand**	**stay**	your
elbows	nose	shake	**stinks**	
elephant	of	**shirt**	the	
everywhere	old	**shoe**	them	

About the Author

Pam Miller is a former preschool teacher. She lives in Gaithersburg, Maryland, with her husband, Lex, and their two children, Chris and Elizabeth. Pam enjoys her family and her writing, and hopes this book will make you smile because smiles make the best wrinkles.

About the Illustrator

Bob Ostrom has always loved to draw. He started illustrating children's books almost fifteen years ago, but has been drawing silly pictures of one kind or another nearly all his life. When Bob's not busy illustrating books he enjoys spending time with his family. Bob lives in North Carolina with his wife Melissa and three children Wil, Charlie, and Mae.